Temple Wilderness

Temple Wilderness

*A Collection of Thoughts and Images
On Our Spiritual Bond with the Earth*

WILLOW CREEK PRESS
MINOCQUA, WISCONSIN

Published by Willow Creek Press

PO Box 147, Minocqua, WI 54548

EDITORS:

Tom Petrie

Kim Leighton

Greg Linder

PHOTOGRAPHERS:

Erwin and Peggy Bauer: pages 2, 10, 19, 23, 25, 27, 37, 45, 48, 52, 55, 58, 61, 62, 65, 66, 68, 76, 79, 94, 96, 98, 102 btm, 103 top, 104 btm, 107, 115, 116, 118, 125, 126, 128, 134, 137, 141, 158, 162, and 171.

Michael H. Francis: pages 5, 13, 14, 15, 16, 20, 21, 22, 28, 30, 34, 39, 41, 71, 75, 80, 83, 87, 88, 100, 102 top, 103 btm, 105, 109, 111, 112, 120, 121, 123, 133, 139, 148, 151, 152, 159, 164, 166, 167, and 159.

George H. Harrison: pages 6, 84, 95, 104 top, and 131.

Ron Spomer: pages 32, 36, 69, 147, 156, 161, and 172.

Kim Leighton: page 38.

Lon E. Lauber: page: 42, 46, 50, 72, 92, 142, and 174.

Jeff Foott: pages 57, 91, 154, and 155.

DESIGN: Patricia Bickner Linder

LIBRARY OF CONGRESS CATALOGING-IN-PUBLICATION DATA

Temple wilderness : a collection of thoughts and images on our spiritual bond with the Earth / [editors, Tom Petrie, Kim Leighton, Greg Linder].
ISBN 1-57223-051-7 (alk. paper)
1. Nature—Religious aspects.   2. Human ecology—Religious aspects.
I. Petrie, Tom.   II. Leighton, Kim.   III. Linder, Greg.
BL65.N35T46   1996
291.2'12—dc20   96-26856
CIP

Contents

1 *Tribal Memories* 7

2 *The Nature of Spirituality* 11

3 *Temple Wilderness* 43

4 *Lessons on the Wind* 89

5 *How Much Are the Birds?* 129

6 *A Child of the Universe* 149

v

1

Tribal Memories

onsider: human advance is determined not by reason alone but by emotions peculiar to our species, aided and tempered by reason. What makes us people and not computers is emotion. We have little grasp of our true nature, of what it is to be human and therefore where our descendants might someday wish we had directed Spaceship Earth. Our troubles, as Vercors said in *You Shall Know Them*, arise from the fact that we do not know what we are and cannot agree on what we want to be. The primary cause of this intellectual failure is ignorance of our origins. We did not arrive on this planet as aliens. Humanity is part of nature, a species that evolved among other species. The more closely we identify ourselves with the rest of life, the more quickly we will be able to discover the sources of human sensibility and acquire the knowledge on which an enduring ethic, a sense of preferred direction, can be built.

The human heritage does not go back only for the conventionally recognized 8,000 years or so of recorded history, but for at least 2 million years, to the appearance of the first "true" human beings, the earliest species composing the genus Homo. Across thousands of generations, the emergence of culture must have been profoundly influenced by simultaneous events in genetic evolution, especially those occurring in the anatomy and physiology of the brain. Conversely, genetic evolution must have been guided forcefully by the kinds of selection rising within culture.

Only in the last moment of human history has the delusion arisen that people can flourish apart from the rest of the living world. Preliterate societies were in intimate contact with a bewildering array of life forms. Their minds could only partly adapt to that challenge. But they struggled to understand the most relevant parts, aware that the right responses gave life and fulfillment, the wrong ones sickness, hunger, and death. The imprint of that effort cannot have been erased in a few generations of urban existence. I suggest that it is to be found among the particularities of human nature, among which are these:

• The favored living place of most peoples is a prominence near water from which parkland can be viewed. On such heights are found the abodes of the powerful and rich, tombs of the great, temples, parliaments, and monuments commemorating tribal glory. The location is today an aesthetic choice and, by the implied freedom to settle there, a symbol of status. In ancient, more practical times the topography provided a place to retreat and a sweeping prospect from which to spot the distant approach of storms and enemy forces. Every animal species selects a habitat in which its members gain a favorable mix of security and food. For most of deep history, human beings lived in tropical and subtropical savanna in East Africa, open country sprinkled with streams and lakes, trees and copses. In similar topography modern peoples choose their residences and design their parks and gardens, if given a free choice. They simulate neither dense jungles, toward which gibbons are drawn, nor dry grasslands, preferred by hamadryas baboons. In their gardens they plant trees that resemble the acacias, sterculias, and other native trees of the African savannas. The ideal tree crown sought is consistently wider than tall, with spreading lowermost branches close enough to the ground to touch and climb, clothed with compound or needle-shaped leaves.

• Given the means and sufficient leisure, a large portion of the populace backpacks, hunts, fishes, birdwatches, and gardens. In the United States and Canada more people visit zoos and aquariums than attend all professional athletic events combined. They crowd the national parks to view natural landscapes, looking from the tops of prominences out across rugged terrain for a glimpse of tumbling water and animals living free. They travel long distances to stroll along the seashore, for reasons they can't put into words.

These are examples of what I have called biophilia, the connections that human beings subconsciously seek with the rest of life. To biophilia can be added the idea of wilderness, all the land and communities of plants and animals still unsullied by human occupation. Into wilderness people travel in search of new life and wonder, and from wilderness they return to the parts of the earth that have been humanized and made physically secure. Wilderness settles peace on the soul because it needs no help; it is beyond human contrivance.

Wilderness is a metaphor of unlimited opportunity, rising from the tribal memory of a time when humanity spread across the world, valley to valley, island to island, godstruck, firm in the belief that virgin land went on forever past the horizon.

I cite these common preferences of mind not as proof of an innate human nature but rather to suggest that we think more carefully and turn philosophy to the central questions of human origins in the wild environment. We do not understand ourselves yet and descend farther from heaven's air if we forget how much the natural world means to us. Signals abound that the loss of life's diversity endangers not just the body but the spirit. If that much is true, the changes occurring now will visit harm on all generations to come.

— EDWARD O. WILSON, *The Diversity of Life*, 1992

2

The Nature of Spirituality

That was not first which is spiritual, but that which is natural; and afterward that which is spiritual.

— 1 Corinthians 15:46

The truth can only be held in your heart. Our
grandparents tell us everything. We don't lie and make
up new rules all the time. God is nature, nature is God.
That is very simple. We have known it from before time.
— NOBLE RED MAN, OGLALA LAKOTA ELDER

 am that living and fiery essence of the divine substance that flows in
the beauty of the fields, I shine in the water, I burn in the sun and
the moon and the stars. Mine is the mysterious force of the invisible
wind. I sustain the breath of all living. I breathe in the verdure, and
in the flowers, and when the waters flow like living things, it is I.
— THE HOLY SPIRIT, IN A VISION TO
SAINT HILDEGARD OF BINGEN

This world is the abode of God,
and God truly lives in the world.
— GURU ANGAD

The whole earth is a thurible heaped with incense, afire with the divine, yet not consumed. This is
the most spiritual of earth's joys — too subtle for analysis, mysteriously connected with light and
with whiteness, for white flowers are the sweetest — yet it penetrates the physical being to its
depths. Here is a symbol of the material value of spiritual things. If we washed our souls in these
healing perfumes as often as we wash our hands, our lives would be infinitely more wholesome.
— MARY WEBB, *Poems and the Spring of Joy*

s soon as we allow ourselves to think of the world as alive, we recognize that a part of us knew this all along. It is like emerging from winter into spring. We can begin to reconnect our mental life with our own direct intuitive experiences of nature. We can participate in the spirits of sacred places and times. We can see that we have much to learn from traditional societies who have never lost their sense of connection with the living world around them. We can acknowledge the animistic traditions of our ancestors. And we can begin to develop a richer understanding of human nature, shaped by tradition, and collective memory, linked to the earth and the heavens, related to all forms of life, and consciously open to the creative power expressed in all evolution. We are reborn into a living world.

— RUPERT SHELDRAKE, *The Rebirth of Nature: The Greening of Science and God*

**A**nd in that unbroken quiet and amidst this bright company of heaven my spirit seemed to become intenser and more daring. Right high up in the zenith, to infinite height, it would soar unfettered. And right round to any distance in any direction it would pierce its way. The height and distance of the highest and farthest stars I knew had been measured. I knew that the resulting number of miles is something so immense as to be altogether beyond human conception. I knew also that the number of stars, besides those few thousands which I saw, had to be numbered in hundreds of millions. All this was astonishing, and the knowledge of it filled me with wonder at the immensity of the Starry Universe. But it was not the mere magnitude of this world that impressed me. What stirred me was the Presence, subtly felt, of some mighty, all-pervading Influence which ordered the courses of the heavenly hosts and permeated every particle.

We cannot watch the sun go down, day after day, and after it has set see the stars appear, rise to the meridian and disappear below the opposite horizon in regular procession without being impressed by the order which prevails. We feel that the whole is kept together in punctual fashion, and is not mere chaos and chance. The presence of some Power upholding, sustaining, and directing the whole is deeply impressed upon us. And in this Presence so steadfast, so calm, so constant, we feel soothed and steadied. The frets and pains of ordinary life are stilled. Deep peace and satisfaction fills our souls.

— SIR FRANCIS YOUNGHUSBAND, *The Heart of Nature*

e have today to learn to get back into accord with the wisdom of nature and realize again our brotherhood with the animals and with the water and the sea ... The idea is trans-theological. It is an undefinable, inconceivable mystery, thought of as a power, that is the source and end and supporting ground of all life and being.

— JOSEPH CAMPBELL, *The Power of Myth*

I swear the earth shall surely be complete to him or
      her who shall be complete,
The earth remains jagged and broken only to him
      or her who remains jagged and broken.
I swear there is no greatness or power that does not
      emulate those of the earth,
There can be no theory of any account unless it
      corroborate the theory of the earth,
No politics, song, religion, behavior, or what not,
      is of account, unless it compare with the
      amplitude of the earth,
Unless it face the exactness, vitality, impartiality,
      rectitude of the earth.

— WALT WHITMAN

 he American Indian is of the soil, whether it be the region of forests, plains, pueblos, or mesas. He fits into the landscape, for the hand that fashioned the continent also fashioned the man for his surroundings. He once grew as naturally as the wild sunflowers; he belongs just as the buffalo belonged ...

— LUTHER STANDING BEAR, OGLALA SIOUX CHIEF

 he indescribable innocence and beneficence of Nature, — of sun and wind and rain, of summer and winter, — such health, such cheer, they afford forever! … Shall I not have intelligence with the earth? Am I not partly leaves and vegetable mould myself?

— HENRY DAVID THOREAU

Earth brings us into life
and nourishes us.
Earth takes us back again.
Birth and death are present in every moment.

— THICH NHAT HANH

hough I do not expect that I shall be reborn directly as a crocus, I know that one day my atoms will inhabit a bacterium here, a diatom there, a nematode or a flagellate — even a crayfish or a sea cucumber. I will be here, in myriad forms, for as long as there are forms of life on Earth. I have always been here, and with a certain effort of will, I can sometimes remember.

— JOHN A. LIVINGSTON, *One Cosmic Instant, A Natural History of Human Arrogance*, 1953

O Lord, Thou art on the sandbanks
As well as in the midst of the current;
I bow to Thee.
Thou art in the little pebbles
As well as in the calm expanse of the sea;
I bow to Thee.
O all-pervading Lord,
Thou art in the barren soil
And in crowded places;
I bow to Thee.

— 'SUKLA YAJUR, VEDA XVI

Nature! We are surrounded and embraced by her; powerless to separate ourselves from her, and powerless to penetrate beyond her ... We live in her midst and know her not. She is incessantly speaking to us, but betrays not her secret ... She has always thought and always thinks; though not as a man, but as Nature ... She loves herself, and her innumerable eyes and affections are fixed upon herself. She has divided herself that she may be her own delight. She causes an endless succession of new capacities for enjoyment to spring up, that her insatiable sympathy may be assuaged ... The spectacle of Nature is always new, for she is always renewing the spectators. Life is her most exquisite invention; and death is her expert contrivance to get plenty of life.

— GOETHE, GERMAN POET, 1869

There is a certain triviality in any spiritual discipline that does not experience itself as supported by the spiritual as well as the physical dynamics of the entire cosmic-earth process. A spirituality is a mode of being in which not only the divine and the human commune with each other, but we discover ourselves in the universe and the universe discovers itself in us. The Sioux Indian Crazy Horse called upon these depths of his being when he invoked the cosmic forces to support himself in battle. He painted the lightning upon his cheek, placed a rock behind his ear, an eagle feather in his hair, and the head of a hawk upon his head. Assumption of the cosmic insignia is also evident in the Sun Dance Ceremony. In this dance the symbols of the sun and moon and stars are cut out of rawhide and worn by the dancers. The world of living moving things is indicated by the form of the buffalo cut from rawhide, and by eagle feathers. The plant world is represented by the cottonwood tree set up in the center of the ceremonial circle. The supreme spirit itself is represented by the circular form of the dance area.

So the spiritual personality should feel constantly in communion with those numinous cosmic forces out of which we were born. Furthermore the cosmic-earth order needs to be supplemented by the entire historical order of human development.

— THOMAS BERRY, *Liberating Life*

he voice of the Great Spirit is heard in the twittering of birds, the rippling of mighty waters, and the sweet breathing of flowers. If this is Paganism, then at present, at least, I am a Pagan.

— ZITKALA-SA, DAKOTA SIOUX

he forces of Nature are something to be felt into, to be reached out to ... sense the Nature forces such as the wind, to perceive its essence ... be positive and harmonize with that essence ... You can cooperate in the garden. Begin by thinking about the nature spirits, the higher overlighting nature spirits, and tune into them. That will be so unusual as to draw their interest here. They will be overjoyed to find some members of the human race eager for their help ... All forces are to be felt into, even the sun, the moon, the sea the trees, the very grass. All are part of my life. All is one life.

— *Chop Wood, Carry Water*

I have heard the elders say that everything in nature has its own spirit and possesses a power beyond ours. There is no way to prove them right or wrong, though the beauty and interrelatedness of things should be evidence enough. We need not ask for shining visions as proof, or for a message from a golden deer glowing in the sky of our dreams. Above all else, we should assume that power moves in the world around us and act accordingly. If it is a myth, then spirit is within the myth and we should live by it. And if there is a commandment to follow, it is to approach all of earth-life, of which we are a part, with humility and respect.

— RICHARD K. NELSON, *On Nature*

The moral Laws form one system with the Laws by which Heaven and Earth support and contain, overshadow and canopy all things. These moral Laws form the same system with the laws by which the seasons succeed each other and the sun and moon appear with the alterations of day and night. It is this same system of Laws by which all created things are produced and develop themselves each in its order and system without injuring one another; by which the operations of nature take their course without conflict and confusion, the Lesser forces flowing everywhere like river currents, while the great forces of creation go silently and steadily on.

It is this — one system running through all — that makes the Universe so impressively great.

— CONFUCIUS

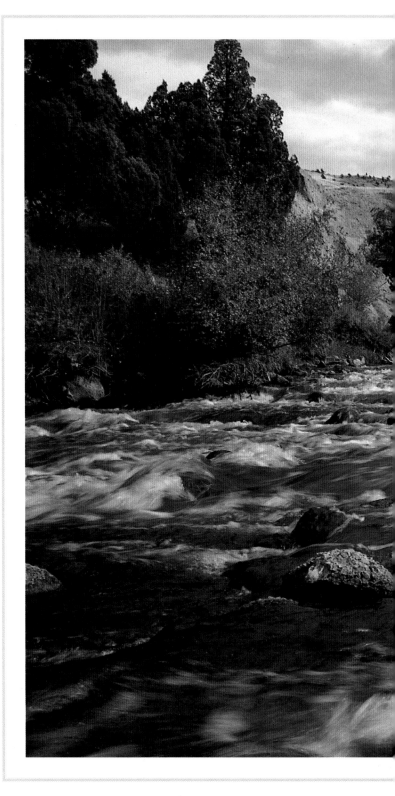

 n nature, there is no such thing as a clash of colors. The more carefully you look, the deeper the subtleties of harmony. It is not so much that things flow into each other or around each other like perfect jigsaw pieces; rather it is that there is only One Thing out there. And somehow, it is not really "out there." Somehow, it is "in here" too. Inside. At the furthest wavelength of thought, the sea and the wind and the trees and sand are . . . me. It is a thought that blinks into the mind, like a giant laughing eye, and then is gone for a long, long time.

— ROBERT HUNTER, *O Seasons, O Castles*

If you will think of ourselves as coming out of the earth, rather than having been thrown in here from somewhere else, you see that we are the earth, we are the consciousness of the earth. These are the eyes of the earth. And this is the voice of the earth. When you see the earth from the moon, you don't see any divisions there of nations or states. This might be the symbol, really, for the new mythology to come.

— JOSEPH CAMPBELL, *The Power of Myth*

The Great Spirit is in all things; he is in the air we breathe.
The Great Spirit is our Father, but the earth is our mother.
She nourishes us; that which we put into the ground she
returns to us . . .

— BIG THUNDER, WABANAKI ALGONQUIN

THE NATURAL ORDER

A man must go wheresoever his parents bid him. Nature is no other than a man's parents. If she bid me die quickly, and I demur, then I am an unfilial son. She can do me no wrong. Tao gives me this form, this toil in manhood, this repose in old age, this rest in death. And surely, that which is such a kind arbiter of my life is the best arbiter of my death.

— CHUANG TZU

A child said *What is the grass?*
   fetching it to me with full hands;
  How could I answer the child?
   I do not know what it is any more than he.
 I guess it must be the flag of my disposition,
  out of hopeful green stuff woven.
 Or I guess it is the handkerchief of the Lord,
 A scented gift and remembrancer designedly dropt,
 Bearing the owner's name someway in the corners,
  that we may see and remark, and say Whose?
    — WALT WHITMAN, *Leaves of Grass*

Grass is as universal as dew, as commonplace as light. It is of all the signatures of nature that which to us is nearest and homeliest. Everywhere and ever has this omnipresent herb, that withereth and yet is continually reborn, been the eternal symbol of that which passes like a dream, the symbol of everlasting illusion, and yet, too, is the symbol of resurrection, of all the old divine illusion essayed anew, of the inexplicable mystery of life recovered and everlastingly perpetuated.

    — FIONA MACLEOD, *At the Turn of the Year*

And now for the Water, the Element that I trade in. The water is the eldest daughter of the Creation, the Element upon which the Spirit of God did first move, the element which God commanded to bring forth living creatures abundantly; and without which those that inhabit the Land, even all creatures that have breath in their nostrils must suddenly return to putrifaction. Moses the great Law-giver and chief Philosopher, skilled in all the learning of the Egyptians, who was called the friend of God, and knew the mind of the Almighty, names this element the first in the Creation; this is the element upon which the Spirit of God did first move, and is the chief Ingredient in the Creation ...

— IZAAK WALTON,
The Compleat Angler

he highest good is like water. Water gives life to the ten thousand things and does not strive.

— LAO TSU

he shore is an ancient world, for as long as there has been an earth and sea there has been this place of the meeting of land and water. Yet it is a world that keeps alive the sense of continuing creation and of the relentless drive of life. Each time that I enter it, I gain some new awareness of its beauty and its deeper meanings, sensing that intricate fabric of life by which one creature is linked with another, and each with its surroundings.

— RACHEL CARSON, *The Edge of the Sea*

 haze on the far horizon,
The infinite, tender sky,
The ripe rich tint of the cornfields
And the wild geese sailing high —
And all over upland and lowland,
The charm of the golden-rod —
Some of us call it Autumn
And others call it God.

— WILLIAM HERBERT CARRUTH,
Each In His Own Tongue

... I put on a dark coat and go out to be a part of the evening, and when I look up I am in the midst of an incredible galaxy of snowflakes. I return to the porch, and under the porch light I see the individual flakes on my coat sleeve. I cannot understand the infinite variety of the snowflakes, but there they are, crystalline perfection so fragile that my slightest breath reduces them to drops of moisture.

I return to the dooryard and stand there in the falling snow. The dusk deepens. Night is at hand. Soon I shall come back inside, to the security of walls and roof and fire, fruit of my own providence. But for a little while I am one with the dark and the snow, and I am full of wonder. Here is wholeness and holiness, and I partake, knowing that beyond the reasons lies belief.

— HAL BORLAND, *Homeland*

hen I was somewhat past ten years of age, my father took me with him to watch the horses out on the prairie ... While we sat watching the herd my father said: "These horses are godlike, or mystery beings."

— WOLF CHIEF, HIDATSA SIOUX

*his grand show is eternal. It is always sunrise somewhere; the dew is never all dried at once; a shower is forever falling; vapor is ever rising. Eternal sunrise, eternal sunset, eternal dawn and gloaming, on sea and continents and islands, each in its turn, as the round earth rolls.*

— JOHN MUIR

For we are of the earth, earth-born and earth-bound. There is nothing to be unhappy about in the fact that we are, as it were, delivered upon this beautiful earth as its transient guests. Even if it were a dark dungeon, we still would have to make the best of it; it would be ungrateful of us not to do so when we have, instead of a dungeon, such a beautiful earth to live on for a good part of a century. Sometimes we get too ambitious and disdain the humble and yet generous earth. Yet a sentiment for this Mother Earth, a feeling of true affection and attachment, one must have for this temporary abode of our body and spirit, if we are to have a sense of spiritual harmony.

— LIN YUTANG, *The Importance of Living*

3
Temple Wilderness

I f we do not go to church so much as did our fathers, we go to the woods much more, and are much more inclined to make a temple of them than our fathers were. We now use the word "Nature" very much as our fathers used the word "God," and I suppose, back of it all we mean the power that is everywhere present and active, and in whose lap the visible universe is held and nourished. It is a power that we can see and touch and hear, and we realize every moment of our lives how absolutely we are dependent upon it. There are no atheists or skeptics in regard to this power. All men see how literally we are its children and all men learn how swift and sure is the penalty of disobedience to its commands. Our associations with Nature vulgarize it and rob it of its divinity. When we come to see that the celestial and the terrestrial are one, that time and eternity are one, that there is nothing not inherent in Nature, then we no longer look for or expect a far-off, unknown God.

Nature teaches more than she preaches. There are no sermons in stones. It is easier to get a spark out of stone than a moral.

— JOHN BURROUGHS, *Time and Change*

Some people talk about finding God — as if He could get lost.

— ANONYMOUS

his temple which the Great Architect has been building for a score of centuries is incomparably nobler, more beautiful and more serene than any erected by the hands of man. Its nave is loftier than that of Amiens and longer than that of St. Peter's. Its wine-red shafts, rising clean and straight over two hundred feet, are more numerous than the pillars of Cordova; its floor is carpeted with a green and brown mosaic more intricate than that of St. Mark's; its aisles are lit with a translucence more beautiful than that which filters through the stained glass of Chartres; its spires pierce higher than those of Cologne; its years are greater than those of the first lowly building devoted to Christian service.

— DUNCAN MCDUFFIE, *The Last Redwoods and the Parkland of Redwood Creek*

Some keep the Sabbath going to church;
I keep it staying at home,
With a bobolink for a chorister,
And an orchard for a dome.

Some keep the Sabbath in surplice;
I just wear my wings,
And instead of tolling the bell for church,
Our little sexton sings.

God preaches, — a noted clergyman, —
And the sermon is never long;
So instead of getting to heaven at last,
I'm going all along!

— EMILY DICKINSON

From the chill, grey peak above, from the everlasting snows, from the silvered pines, down through mountain ranges with their depths of Tyrian purple, we looked to where the Plains lay cold, in blue-grey, like a morning sea against a far horizon. Suddenly, as a dazzling streak at first, but enlarging rapidly into a dazzling sphere, the sun wheeled above the grey line, a light and glory as when it was first created. Jim involuntarily and reverently uncovered his head, and exclaimed, "I believe there is a God!"

— ISABELLA BIRD,
A Lady's Life in the Rocky Mountains

o look upon that landscape in the early morning ... is to lose the sense of proportion. Your imagination comes to life, and this, you think, is where Creation was begun.

— N. SCOTT MOMADAY,
KIOWA INDIAN AND
PULITZER PRIZE WINNER

46

In the beginning God created the heaven and the earth

… And God saw everything that he had made, and behold, it was very good.

— Genesis 1

Then he realized, I indeed, I am this creation, for I have poured it forth from myself. In that way he became this creation. Verily, he who knows this becomes in this creation a creator.

— Hindu Upanishads

And the Spirit of God was moving over the face of the waters. And God said, "Let there be light"; and there was light.

— Genesis I

n the beginning, there was only the great self reflected in the form of a person. Reflecting, it found nothing but itself. Then its first word was, "This am I."

— Hindu Upanishads

Aditya (the sun) is Brahman, this is the doctrine, and this is the fuller account of it: —

In the beginning this was non-existent. It became existent, it grew. It turned into an egg. The egg lay for the time of a year.

The egg broke open. The two halves were one of silver, the other of gold.

The silver one became this earth, the golden one the sky, the thick membrane (of the white) the mountains, the thin membrane (of the yolk) the mist with the clouds, the small veins the rivers, the fluid the sea.

And what was born from it that was Aditya, the sun. When he was born shouts of hurrah arose, and all beings arose, and all things which they desired. Therefore whenever the sun rises and sets, shouts of hurrah arise, and all beings arise, and all things which they desire.

If any one knowing this meditates on the sun as Brahman, pleasant shouts will approach him and will continue, yea, they will continue.

— Nineteenth Khanda

As if it were the moment before the actual instant of creation, the last second before the awesome command: Let there be light!

I never feel so alone in the world, completely uprooted and at the same time completely soothed, so tense with yearning and at the same time, blissfully certain of ultimate fulfillment as in this hour before dawn and day.

— FELIX SALTEN, *Good Comrades*

The day has risen,
Go I to behold the dawn,
Hao! you maidens!
Go behold the dawn!
The white-rising!
The yellow-rising!
It has become light.

— HOPI SONG

When you arise in the morning,
give thanks for the morning light,
for your life and strength.
Give thanks for your food
and the joy of living.
If you see no reason for giving thanks,
the fault lies in yourself.

— TECUMSEH

Eagle soaring, see the morning
see the new mysterious morning
something marvelous and sacred
though it happens every day
Dawn the child of God and Darkness

— PAWNEE PRAYER

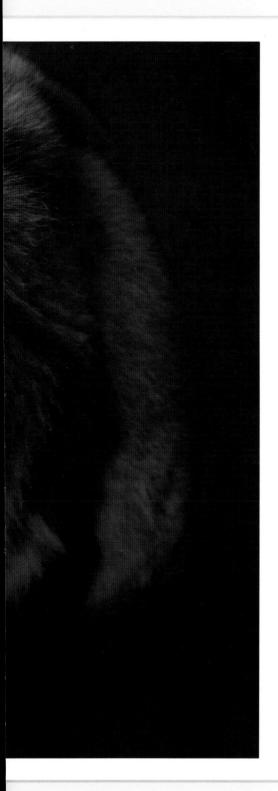

THE TIGER

Tiger, Tiger, burning bright
In the forests of the night;
What immortal hand or eye,
Could frame thy fearful symmetry?

In what distant deeps or skies
Burnt the fire of thine eyes!
On what wings dare he aspire?
What the hand, dare seize the fire?

And what shoulder, & what art,
Could twist the sinews of thy heart?
And when thy heart began to beat,
What dread hand? & what dread feet?

What the hammer? what the chain?
In what furnace was thy brain?
What the anvil? what dread grasp
Dare its deadly terrors clasp?

When the stars threw down their spears
And water'd heaven with their tears:
Did he smile his work to see?
Did he who made the Lamb make thee?

Tiger, Tiger, burning bright,
In the forests of the night:
What immortal hand or eye,
Dare frame thy fearful symmetry?

— WILLIAM BLAKE

The evolution of the world is a great manifestation of God. As scientists understand more and more about the interdependence not only of living things but of rocks, rivers — the whole of the universe — I am left in awe that I, too, am a part of this tremendous miracle. Not only am I a part of this pulsating network, but I am an indispensable part. It is not only theology that teaches me this, but it is the truth that environmentalists shout from the rooftops. Every living creature is an essential part of the whole …

Our surroundings are awesome. We see about us majestic mountains, the perfection of a tiny mouse, a newborn baby, a flower, the colors of a seashell. Each creature is most fully that which it is created to be, an almost incredible reflection of the infinite, the invisible, the indefinable. All women and men participate in that reflected glory.

— DESMOND TUTU, *The Meaning of Life*

The force that through the green fuse drives the flower
Drives my green age, that blasts the roots of trees
Is my destroyer.
And I am dumb to tell the crooked rose
My youth is bent by the same wintry fever.

— DYLAN THOMAS

hou art the dark blue bird, and the green parrot with red eyes. Thou hast the lightning as thy child. Thou art the season and the seas. Having no beginning, thou dost abide with immanence, whereof all things are born.

— *Upanishads*

THE GREAT WORKS OF HIS HANDS

We magnify thee, O Lord almighty, we bless the excellency of thy name in the great works of thy hands, the manifold beauties of earth and sky and sea, the courses of the stars and light, the songs of birds, the hues of flowers, the diversity of all living creatures, and, upholding all, thy wisdom, marvelous worthy to be praised; but most, that by thy sure promise we now do only taste the glory that shall be revealed, when thou, O God, wilt take the power and reign; world without end.

— *Book of Common Prayer*, CHURCH OF INDIA, PAKISTAN, BURMA AND CEYLON

 less the waters that flow through our land.
Fill them with fish and drive great schools of fish to our seacoast,
so that the fishermen in their unsteady boats
do not need to go out too far.

— ASHANTI PRAYER

I thank You God for most this amazing
day: for the leaping greenly spirit of trees
and a blue true dream of sky; and for everything
which is natural which is infinite which is yes.

— E.E. CUMMINGS

You see, the whole world is praying all the time. The animals and even the leaves on the trees are praying. The way to receive light from God is through praying.

— SCHLOMO CARLBACH

HOW GREAT THOU ART

O Lord, my God! When I in awesome wonder
Consider all the worlds Thy hands have made,
I see the stars, I hear the rolling thunder,
Thy power throughout the universe displayed,

When through the woods and forest glades I wander
And hear the birds sing sweetly in the trees;
When I look down from lofty mountain grandeur
And hear the brook and feel the gentle breeze,

Then sings my soul, my Saviour God, to Thee.
How great Thou art, how great Thou art!
Then sings my soul, my Saviour God, to Thee.
How great Thou art, how great Thou art!

— STUART K. HINE

For the Lord your God is bringing you into a great
*   land,*
a land of flowing streams, with springs and
*   underground waters welling up in the valleys*
*   and hills.*
You can eat your fill and bless the Lord your God for
*   the good land he has given you.*

— Deuteronomy

Be praised, my Lord. with all your creatures, especially master brother sun, who brings day,
and you give us light by him . . .
Be praised, my Lord, for sister moon and the stars, in heaven you have made them clear and
precious and lovely.
Be praised, my Lord, for brother wind and for the air, cloudy and fair and in all weathers —
by which you give sustenance to your creatures.
Be praised, my Lord, for sister water, who is very useful and humble and rare and chaste.
Be praised, my Lord, for brother fire . . .
Be praised, my Lord, for sister our mother earth . . .

— ST. FRANCIS OF ASSISI

And God said, "Behold I have given you every plant yielding seed which is on the face of all the
earth and every tree yielding seed in its fruit: you shall have them for food. And to every beast of
the earth, and to every bird of the air, and to everything that creeps on the earth, everything that
has the breath of life, I have given every green plant for food."

— *Genesis*

The earth is the Lord's and the fullness thereof.

— *Psalm 24:1*

*he earth is full of thy riches*

— *Psalm 104:24*

Blessed of the Lord be his land . . . for the precious
things of the earth and fullness thereof.

— *Deut. 33:13, 16*

looked out at the icebergs.
They were so beautiful they
also made you afraid.

— BARRY LOPEZ,
Arctic Dreams

How wonderful, O Lord, are the works of your hands!
The heavens declare Your glory,
　　the arch of sky displays Your handiwork.
In Your love You have given us the power
　　to behold the beauty of Your world
　　robed in all its splendor.
The sun and the stars, the valleys and hills,
　　the rivers and lakes all disclose Your presence.
The roaring breakers of the sea tell of Your awesome might;
　　the beasts of the field and the birds of the air
　　bespeak Your wondrous will.
In Your goodness You have made us able to hear
　　the music of the world. The voices of loved ones
　　reveal to us that You are in our midst.
A divine voice sings through all creation.

— JEWISH PRAYER

 *hen weave for us a garment of brightness.*
May the warp be the white light of morning,
May the weft be the red light of evening,
May the fringes be the falling rain,
May the border be the standing rainbow,
Thus weave for us a garment of brightness,
That we may walk fittingly where birds sing,
That we may walk fittingly where grass is green,
O our Mother the Earth,
Our Father the Sky.

— KENNETH LINCOLN, *The Good Red Road*

here is a river, the streams whereof shall make glad the city of God, the holy place of the tabernacles of the most High.

God is in the midst of her; she shall not be moved: God shall help her, and that right early.

— *Psalm 46*

*S*ilently a flower blooms, In silence it falls away;
Yet here now, at this moment, at this place,
The world of the flower, the whole of
    the world is blooming.
This is the talk of the flower, the truth
    of the blossom;
The glory of eternal life is fully shining here.

           — ZENKEI SHIBAYAMA

he earth rolls upon her wings, and the sun giveth his light by day,
and the moon giveth her light by night,
and the stars also give their light, as they roll upon their wings in their glory,
in the midst of the power of God.

Unto what shall I liken these kingdoms that ye may understand?

Behold all these are kingdoms and any man who hath seen any of the least
of these hath seen God moving in his majesty and power.
— MORMON SCRIPTURE, *Doctrine and Covenants* 88:44-47

... Standing quietly on the ice, a few feet from shore, I heard a low, muffled moan — a full but dim resonance, like a grouse drumming, or like a night wind in the eaves. At first I thought it was the echo of a distant explosion. Then I felt a vibration beneath my feet. It was the ice.

Again and again, the ice sheet groaned. The rumble echoed off the trees, punctuated now and then by a sharp crack. As my ears adjusted I heard other, distant groanings — the expanding ice of nearby lakes. In deep winter the snow muffles the eerie music of the ice, but on this night all the lakes were cold and bare. I was listening to a symphony of freezing lakes, massive sheets of ice releasing the stress of their growth in heaving cracks that wailed softly in birth. It transfixed me with its simple, awesome power. Nothing that any man could ever do would change the tune of the ice.

— PETER M. LESCHAK, *Letters from Side Lake*

 o see a world in a grain of sand
And heaven in a wild flower
Hold infinity in the palm of your hand
And eternity in an hour.

— WILLIAM BLAKE

WHEN I HEARD THE LEARN'D ASTRONOMER

hen I heard the learn'd astronomer,
When the proofs, the figures, were ranged in columns before me,
When I was shown the charts and diagrams, to add, divide, and
     measure them
When I sitting heard the astronomer where he lectured with much applause in
     the lecture-room,
How soon unaccountable I became tired and sick,
Till rising and gliding out I wander'd off by myself,
In the mystical moist night-air, and from time to time,
Look'd up in perfect silence at the stars.

— WALT WHITMAN

When a man does a piece of work which is admired by all we say that it is
wonderful; but when we see the changes of day and night, the sun, the moon, and
the stars in the sky, and the changing seasons upon the earth, with their ripening
fruits, anyone must realize that it is the work of someone more powerful than man.

— CHASED-BY-BEARS, SANTEE-YANKTONAI SIOUX

I believe a leaf of grass is no less than the journey-work of the stars,
And the pismire (ant) is equally perfect, and a grain of sand, and the egg of the wren,
And the tree-toad is a chef-d'oeuvre for the highest,
And the running blackberry would adorn the parlors of heaven,
And the narrowest hinge in my hand puts to scorn all machinery,
And the cow crunching with depress'd head surpasses any statue,
And a mouse is miracle enough to stagger sextillions of infidels.

— WALT WHITMAN

*Several days after looking at the Earth a childish thought occurred to me —
that we cosmonauts are being deceived.*

*If we are the first ones in space, then who was it who made the globe
correctly? Then this thought was replaced by pride in the human capacity to
see with our mind.*

— RUSSIAN COSMONAUT IGOR VOLK

*Gaia, as I see her, is no doting mother tolerant of misdemeanours,
nor is she some fragile and delicate damsel in danger from brutal
mankind. She is stern and tough, always keeping the world warm
and comfortable for those who obey the rules, but ruthless in her
destruction of those who transgress.*

— JAMES LOVELOCK, *The Age of Gaia*

I saw only the noble earth on which I was born, with the great Star which warms
and enlightens it. I saw the clouds that hand their significant drapery over us. It
was Day — that was all Heaven said. The pines glittered with their innumerable
green needles in the light, and seemed to challenge me to read their riddle. The
drab oak-leaves of the last year turned their little somersets and lay still again.
And the wind bustled high overhead in the forest top. This gay and grand
architecture, from the vault to the moss and lichen on which I lay, — who shall
explain to me the laws of its proportion and adornments?

— RALPH WALDO EMERSON, *The Journals of Ralph Waldo Emerson*

here the forest murmurs there is music: ancient, everlasting. Go to the winter woods: listen there, look, watch, and "the dead months" will give you a subtler secret than any you have yet found in the forest. There is always one possible superb fortune. You may see the woods in snow. There is nothing in the world more beautiful than the forest clothed to its very hollows in snow. That is loveliness to which surely none can be insensitive. It is the still ecstasy of Nature, wherein every spray, every blade of grass, every spire of reed, every intricacy of twig, is clad with radiance, and myriad form is renewed in continual change as though in the passionate delight of the white Artificer. It is beauty so great and complex that the imagination is stilled into an aching hush.

— FIONA MACLEOD, *Where the Forest Murmurs*

THIS COMPOST

omething startles me where I thought I was safest,
I withdraw from the still woods I loved,
I will not go now on the pastures to walk,
I will not strip the clothes from my body to meet my lover the sea,
I will not touch my flesh to the earth as to other flesh to renew.

O how can it be that the ground itself does not sicken? How can you be
    alive you growths of spring?
How can you furnish health you blood of herbs, roots, orchards, grain?
Are they not continually putting distemper'd corpses within you?
Is not every continent work'd over and over with sour dead?

Where have you disposed of their carcasses?

Those drunkards and gluttons of so many generations?

Where have you drawn off all the foul liquid and meat?

I do not see any of it upon you today, or perhaps I am deceiv'd,

I will run a furrow with my plough, I will press my spade through the sod and turn it up underneath,

I am sure I shall expose some of the foul meat.

Behold this compost! behold it well!

Perhaps every mite has once form'd part of a sick person — yet behold!

The grass of spring covers the prairies,

The bean bursts noiselessly through the mould in the garden,

The delicate spear of the onion pierces upward,

The apple-buds cluster together on the apple-branches,

The resurrection of the wheat appears with pale visage out of its graves,

The tinge awakes over the willow-tree and the mulberry-tree,

The he-birds carol mornings and evenings while the she-birds sit on their nests,

The young of poultry break through the hatch'd eggs,

The new-born of animals appear, the calf is dropt from the cow, the colt from the mare,

Out of its little hill faithfully rise the potato's dark green leaves,

Out of its hill rises the yellow maize-stalk, the lilacs bloom in the dooryards,

The summer growth is innocent and disdainful above all those strata of sour dead.

What chemistry!

That the winds are really not infectious,

That this is no cheat, this transparent green-wash of the sea which is so amorous after me,

That it is safe to allow it to lick my naked body all over with its tongues,

That it will not endanger me with the fevers that have deposited themselves in it,

That all is clean forever and forever,

That the cool drink from the well tastes so good,

That blackberries are so flavorous and juicy,

That the fruits of the apple-orchard and the orange-orchard, that melons, grapes, peaches,
  plums, will none of them poison me,

That when I recline on the grass I do not catch any disease,

Though probably every spear of grass rises out of what was once a catching disease.

Now I am terrified at the Earth, it is that calm and patient,

It grows such sweet things out of such corruptions,

It turns harmless and stainless on its axis, with such endless successions of diseas'd
  corpses,

It distills such exquisite winds out of such infused fetor,

It renews with such unwitting looks its prodigal, annual, sumptuous crops,

It gives such divine materials to men, and accepts such leavings from them at last.

— WALT WHITMAN

 *All flesh is grass, and all the goodliness
thereof is as the flower of the field.*
— *Isaiah, 40:6*

*The shape of a new mountain is roughly pyramidal,
running out into long shark-finned ridges that
interfere and merge into other thunder-splintered
sierras. You get the saw-tooth effect from a distance,
but the nearby granite bulk glitters with the terrible
keen polish of old glacial ages. I say terrible; so it
seems. When those glossy domes swim into the
alpenglow, wet after rain, you conceive how long and
imperturbable are the purposes of God.*

— MARY AUSTIN, *The Land of Little Rain*

 ow came the solemn, silent evening.
Long, blue, spiky shadows crept out
across the snow-fields, while a rosy
glow, at first scarce discernible,
gradually deepened and suffused every mountain-
top, flushing the glaciers and the harsh crags above
them. This was the alpenglow, to me one of the most
impressive of all the terrestrial manifestations of
God. At the touch of this divine light, the mountains
seemed to kindle to a rapt, religious consciousness,
and stood hushed and waiting like devout wor-
shipers. Just before the alpenglow began to fade, two
crimson clouds came streaming across the summit
like wings of flame, rendering the sublime scene yet
more impressive; then came darkness and the stars.

— JOHN MUIR, *The Mountains of California*

The redwoods, once seen, leave a mark or create a vision that stays with you always. No one has ever successfully painted or photographed a redwood tree. The feeling they produce is not transferable. From them comes silence and awe. It's not only their unbelievable stature, nor the color which seems to shift and vary under your eyes, no, they are not like any trees we know, they are ambassadors from another time.

— JOHN STEINBECK, *Travels with Charley*

I need, so I am told, a faith, something outside of myself to which I can be loyal. And with that I agree, in my own way. I am on what I call "our side," and I know, though vaguely, what I think that is. Wordsworth's God had his dwelling in the light of setting suns. But the God who dwells there seems to me most probably the God of the atom, the star, and the crystal. Mine, if I have one, reveals Himself in another class of phenomena. He makes the grass green and the blood red.

— JOSEPH WOOD KRUTCH, *Two Worlds*

he beauty of the trees, the softness of the air, the fragrance of the grass, speaks to me.
The summit of the mountain, the thunder of the sky, the rhythm of the sea, speaks to me.
The faintness of the stars, the freshness of the morning, the dewdrop on the flower, speaks to me.
The strength of fire, the taste of salmon, the trail of the sun, and the life that never goes away,
    they speak to me.
And my heart soars.

— CHIEF DAN GEORGE

Nature was all in all; we worshipped her and her wordless messages in our hearts were sweeter than honey and the honeycomb.

— W.H. HUDSON, *A Traveller in Little Things*

Hear me, four quarters of the world — a relative I am! Give me the strength to walk the soft earth, a relative to all that is! Give me the eyes to see and the strength to understand, that I may be like you. With your power only can I face the winds.

— BLACK ELK, OGLALA SIOUX HOLY MAN

O Holy One, I ran through the fields and gathered flowers of a
thousand colors—
And now I pour them at Your feet.
Their beauty and their brightness shout for joy in Your Presence.

— ISHPRIYA R.S.C.J.

atanjali, Buddha, Moses and Jesus did not go to workshops or seminars or even churches. They went directly to nature: sat under a Bodhi tree or on top of a mountain or in a cave. We've been living off the residual remains of their inspiration for thousands of years, but this has about run out. It is time to return to the source of this inspiration — the earth itself.

— DOLORES LACHAPELLE, *Earth Wisdom*

Great Spirit
Whose voice I hear in the winds,
 and whose breath gives life to all the world,
 hear me! I am small and weak, I need your strength and wisdom.
Let me walk in beauty, and make my eyes
 ever behold the red and purple sunset.
Make my hands respect the things you have made
 and my ears sharp to hear your voice.
Make me wise so that I may understand the things
 you have taught my people.
Let me learn the lessons you have hidden in every leaf and rock.
I seek strength, not to be greater than my brother,
 but to fight my greatest enemy — myself.
Make me always ready to come to you with clean hands and straight eyes.
So when life fades, as the fading sunset,
 my spirit may come to you without shame.

— TRADITIONAL NATIVE AMERICAN PRAYER

Lord, make this world to last as long as possible.
— PRAYER OF AN 11-YEAR-OLD CHILD ON HEARING OF SINO-INDIAN BORDER FIGHTING

4
Lessons on the Wind

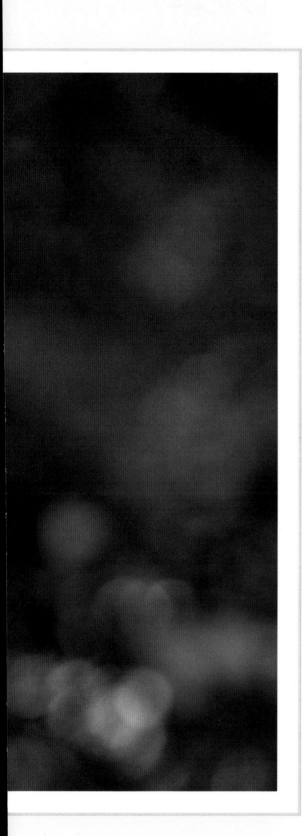

peak to the earth,
and it shall teach thee.
— Job 12:8

I have noticed in my life that all men have a liking for some special animal, tree, plant or spot of earth. If men would pay more attention to these preferences and seek what is best to do in order to make themselves worthy of that toward which they are so attracted, they might have dreams which would purify their lives. Let a man decide upon his favorite animal and make a study of it, learning its innocent ways. Let him learn to understand its sounds and motions. The animals want to communicate with man, but Wakantanka does not intend they shall do so directly — man must do the greater part in securing an understanding.

— BRAVE BUFFALO, TETON SIOUX MEDICINE MAN

ut ask now the beasts,
and they shall teach thee;
and the fowls of the air,
and they shall teach thee;
Or speak to the earth,
and it shall teach thee;
And the fishes of the sea
shall declare unto thee.

— JOB 12:7-8

*In the beginning of all things, wisdom and knowledge were with the animal.
For Tirawa, the One Above, did not speak directly to man. He sent certain
animals to tell mankind that he showed himself through the beast. And that
from them, and from the stars and the sun and the moon, man should learn.*

— A·PAWNEE INDIAN

*There are forces in the woods, forces in the world, that lay claim to you, that lay
a hand on your shoulder so gently that you do not even feel it: not at first. All of
the smallest elements — the direction of a breeze one day, a single sentence that
a friend might speak to you, a raven flying across the meadow and circling back
again — lay claim to you, eventually, with a cumulative power.*

— RICK BASS, *Winter: Notes From Montana*

*Talk of mysteries! Think of our life in nature, — daily to be
shown matter, to come in contact with it, — rocks, trees, wind
on our cheeks! The solid earth! The actual world! The common
sense! Contact! Contact! Who are we? Where are we?*

— HENRY DAVID THOREAU, *The Maine Woods*

*limb the mountains and get their good tidings. Nature's peace will flow into
you as sunshine flows into trees. The winds will blow their own freshness into
you, and the storms their energy, while cares will drop off like autumn leaves.*

— EDWIN WAY TEALE, *The Wilderness World of John Muir*

 ave you gazed on naked grandeur where
there's nothing else to gaze on,
Set pieces and drop-curtain scenes galore,
Big mountains heaved to heaven, which the
blinding sunsets blazon?

Black canyons where the rapids rip and roar?
Have you swept the visioned valley with the green stream streaking through it,
Searched the Vastness for a something you have lost?
Have you strung your soul to silence? Then for God's sake go and do it;
Hear the challenge, learn the lesson, pay the cost.

— ROBERT SERVICE

At the gates of the forest, the surprised man of the world is forced to leave his city estimates of great and small, wise and foolish. The knapsack of custom falls off his back with the first step he makes into these precincts. Here is sanctity which shames our religions, and reality which discredits our heroes. Here we find nature to be the circumstance which dwarfs every other circumstance, and judges like a god all men that come to her ...

It seems as if the day was not wholly profane, in which we have given heed to some natural object.

— RALPH WALDO EMERSON, *Nature*

 hen I was a young man I went to a medicine-man for advice concerning my future. The medicine-man said: "I have not much to tell you except to help you understand this earth on which you live. If a man is to succeed on the hunt or the warpath, he must not be governed by his inclination, but by an understanding of the ways of animals and of his natural surroundings, gained through close observation. The earth is large, and on it live many animals. The earth is under the protection of something which at times becomes visible to the eye."

— ISNA LA-WICA, TETON SIOUX

LEISURE

What is this life if, full of care,
We have no time to stand and stare.

No time to stand beneath the boughs
And stare as long as sheep or cows.

No time to see, when woods we pass,
Where squirrels hide their nuts in grass.

No time to see, in broad daylight,
Streams full of stars like skies at night.

No time to turn at Beauty's glance,
And watch her feet, how they can dance.

No time to wait till her mouth can
Enrich that smile her eyes began.

A poor life this if, full of care,
We have no time to stand and stare.

— WILLIAM HENRY DAVIES

here was a [hermit] who was grazing with the antelopes and who prayed to God, saying, "Lord, teach me something more." And a voice came to him, saying, "Go into this [monastery] and do whatever they command you."

He went there and remained in the [monastery], but did not know the work of the brothers. The young monks began to teach him the work of the brothers and would say to him, "Do this, you idiot," and "Do that, you old fool." And suffering he prayed to God, saying, "Lord I do not know the work of men, send me back to the antelopes." And having been freed by God, he went back into the country to graze with the antelopes.

— The World of the Desert Fathers

... To "be" the wind, stirring up deep waters, requires a leap of imagination, an expansion of mind which cannot fail to attain a level of transcendence. Through the ritual of observation — looking, touching, listening — we come to know the world. One is not enlightened by doing obeisance, by paying dues, but rather by paying attention.

— PETER M. LESCHAK, *Letters from Side Lake*

Man, do not pride yourself on superiority to animals; they are without sin, and you, with your greatness, defile the earth by your appearance on it, and leave the traces of your foulness after you— alas; it is true of almost every one of us!

— FYODOR DOSTOYEVSKY

The exceeding beauty of the earth, in her splendour of life, yields a new thought with every petal. The hours when the mind is absorbed by beauty are the only hours when we really live, so that the longer we can stay among these things so much the more is snatched from inevitable Time ...

To be beautiful and to be calm, without mental fear, is the ideal of nature. If I cannot achieve it, at least I can think it.

— RICHARD JEFFERIES, *The Life of the Fields*

n the landscape of the soul there is a desert, a wilderness, an emptiness, and all great singers must cross this desert to reach the beginning of their road. Jesus. Buddha. Moses. Mohammed. All wandered through the wasteland, speaking to demons, speaking to empty air, listening to the wind, before finding their dove, their bo tree, their stone tablets, before finding their true voice.

— RAY FARADAY NELSON

The first step toward rediscovering this spiritual fountainhead is simple: go out and observe the natural world. We need simply to look very closely. In this way the earth teaches us its eternal message, quietly, in a way unlike the textbook learning about nature.

— *Chop Wood, Carry Water*

We call upon the earth, our planet home, with its beautiful depths and soaring
heights, its vitality and abundance of life, and together we ask that it

Teach us, and show us the Way.

We call upon the mountains, the Cascades and the Olympics, the high green
valleys and meadows filled with wild flowers, the snows that never melt, the
summits of intense silence, and we ask that they

Teach us, and show us the Way.

We call upon the waters that rim the earth, horizon to horizon, that flow in our rivers and streams, that fall upon our gardens and fields and we ask that they

Teach us, and show us the Way.

We call upon the land which grows our food, the nurturing soil, the fertile fields, the abundant gardens and orchards, and we ask that they

Teach us, and show us the Way.

We call upon the forests, the great trees reaching strongly to the sky with earth
in their roots and the heavens in their branches, the fir and the pine
and the cedar, and we ask them to

Teach us, and show us the Way.

We call upon the creatures of the fields and forests and the seas, our brothers and sisters
the wolves and deer, the eagle and dove, the great whales and the dolphin, the beautiful
Orca and salmon who share our Northwest home, and we ask them to

Teach us, and show us the Way.

We call upon all those who have lived on this earth, our ancestors and our friends,
who dreamed the best for future generations, and upon whose lives our lives
are built, and with thanksgiving, we call upon them to

Teach us, and show us the Way.

And lastly, we call upon all that we hold most sacred, the presence and power
of the Great Spirit of love and truth which Rows through
all the Universe ... to be with us to

Teach us, and show us the Way.

— CHINOOK BLESSING LITANY

It's strange to kill your dance partners. But that's what we did. We did it because the world is strange — because this is a world where no matter who you are or where you live or what you eat or whether you choose or don't choose to understand and be grateful, it is sacrifice — sweet bleeding sacrifice — that sustains you. So we killed two trout, but knew no sacrificial prayers, and so simply knelt by the river, commended them on how well they'd fought, whispered,"Swim little soul. Go be a bird, or a singing mouse, or a whale," then broke their bodies to sustain our own.

— JAMES DAVID DUNCAN, *The River Why*

*n our family, there was no clear line between religion and fly fishing. We lived at the junction of great trout rivers in western Montana, and our father was a Presbyterian minister and a fly fisherman who tied his own flies and taught others. He told us about Christ's disciples being fishermen, and we were left to assume, as my brother and I did, that all first-class fishermen on the Sea of Galilee were fly fishermen and that John, the favorite, was a dry-fly fisherman.*

— NORMAN MACLEAN, *A River Runs Through It*

In the first faint gray of the dawn the stately wild turkeys would be stalking around in great flocks, and ready to be sociable and answer invitations to come and converse with other excursionists of their kind. The hunter concealed himself and imitated the turkey-call by sucking the air through the legbone of a turkey which had previously answered a call like that and lived only just long enough to regret it. There is nothing that furnishes a perfect turkey-call except that bone. Another of Nature's treacheries, you see. She is full of them; half the time she doesn't know which she likes best — to betray her child or protect it.

— MARK TWAIN

Never ask your teachers to explain. But when your activity of mind is exhausted and your capacity for feeling comes to a dead end, if something should take place not unlike the cat springing upon the mouse, or the mother hen hatching her eggs, then a great flash of livingness surges up. This is the moment when the phoenix escapes from the golden net and when the crane breaks the bars of its cage.

— HAKUIN, 18TH CENTURY

 *hat is life? It is the flash of a firefly in the night. It is the breath of a buffalo in the winter time. It is the little shadow which runs across the grass and loses itself in the Sunset.*

— CROWFOOT

LOST

Miles from here, in the mountains
There is no sound but snowfall.

The wind rubs itself against the trees
Under its breath

If a crow calls it is nothing
If a branch breaks it is nothing.

The birches look at themselves in the water,
The long white poles of their bodies waver

And bend a little,
The yellow leaves of their hair

Like pieces of far off stars come falling,
Hissing onto the lake

That is smooth as pewter, that is clear
And tranquil as an eye

Lost up here in the mountains
As if someone had dropped it, but no

The pebbles beneath the surface
Have no nerves, they are calm

If a fish leaps it is nothing
Surrounded by moss and blueberries

Flowers breathe among the rocks
So quietly you forget everything

Up here on the crusty grass
The bushes sparkle with ice

And no footprints anywhere,
If a twig snaps it is nothing

For nothing matters, once you have lost it
Down here in the valleys among the people

The sidewalks are full of holes,
Faint memories of far off lakes

Up there in the mountains,
In the great evergreen forests

If a woodchuck whirrs it is nothing,
If a bluejay shrieks it is nothing,

Pine needles slip from the trees, silently
They pile up on the ground.

— PATRICIA GOEDICKE,
The Tongues We Speak: New and Selected Poems

 deep chesty bawl echoes from rimrock to rimrock, rolls down the mountain, and fades into the far blackness of the night. It is an outburst of wild defiant sorrow, and of contempt for all the adversities of the world.

Every living thing (and perhaps many a dead one as well) pays heed to that call. To the deer it is a reminder of the way of all flesh, to the pine a forecast of midnight scuffles and blood upon the snow, to the coyote a promise of gleanings to come, to the cowman a threat of red ink at the bank ... Yet behind these obvious and immediate hopes and fears there lies a deeper meaning, known only to the mountain itself. Only the mountain has lived long enough to listen objectively to the howl of a wolf.

— ALDO LEOPOLD, *A Sand County Almanac*

hen one thinks like a
mountain, one thinks also
like the black bear, so that
honey dribbles down your
fur as you catch the bus to work.
— ROBERT AITKEN, *The Mind of Clover:*
Essays in Zen Buddhist Ethics

When you walk across the fields with your
mind pure and holy,
then from all the stones, and all growing
things, and all animals,
the sparks of their soul come out and cling
to you, and then they
are purified and become a holy fire in you.
— HASIDIC SAYING

113

What would it be like to live in this place? Could a man ever grow weary of such a home? Someday, I thought, I shall make the experiment, become an ancient baldheaded troglodyte with a dirty white beard tucked in my belt, be a shaman, a wizard, a witch doctor crazy with solitude, starving on locusts and lizards, feasting from time to time upon a lost straggler boy scout.

Madness: of course a man would go mad from the beauty and the loneliness, both equally mysterious. But perhaps it would be — who can say? — a kind of blessed insanity, like the bliss of a snake in the winter sun, a buzzard on the summer air.

— EDWARD ABBEY, *Slickrock*

I'm supposed to be a hermit, but what a half-assed hermit I'm turning into: running away to the woods in order to discover that I love people, friends.

But I love the woods too. They're right outside the window. I'm touching my fingers to the cold window panes of the greenhouse. There are wild things just beyond, in the woods. Those wild things — and they are watching me, though I cannot see them, though I see their tracks in the snow — understand my fluttering eyelid, my fluttering heart.

— RICK BASS, *Winter: Notes From Montana*

 umility before the flower at the timber line is the gate which gives access to the path up the open fell.

— DAG HAMMARSKJÖLD, *Markings*

114

Once in a lifetime, perhaps, one escapes the actual confines of the flesh. Once in a lifetime, if one is lucky, one so merges with sunlight and air and running water that whole eons, the eons that mountains and deserts know, might pass in a single afternoon without discomfort. The mind has sunk away into its beginnings among old roots and the obscure tricklings and movings that stir inanimate things. Like the charmed fairy circle into which a man once stepped, and upon emergence learned that a whole century had passed in a single night, one can never quite define this secret; but it has something to do, I am sure, with common water. Its substance reaches everywhere; it touches the past and prepares the future; it moves under the poles and wanders thinly in the heights of air. It can assume forms of exquisite perfection in a snowflake, or strip the living thing to a single shining bone cast up by the sea.

— LOREN EISELEY, *The Immense Journey*

If you love it enough, anything will talk to you.
— GEORGE WASHINGTON CARVER

… Having looked in vain over the pond for a loon, suddenly one, sailing out from the shore toward the middle a few rods in front of me, set up his wild laugh and betrayed himself. I pursued with a paddle and he dived, but when he came up I was nearer than before. He dived again, but I miscalculated the direction he would take, and we were fifty rods apart when he came to the surface this time, for I had helped to widen the interval; and again he laughed long and loud, and with more reason than before …

His usual note was this demoniac laughter, yet somewhat like that of a water-fowl; but occasionally, when he had balked me most successfully and come up a long way off, he uttered a long-drawn unearthly howl, probably more like that of a wolf than any bird; as when a beast puts his muzzle to the ground and deliberately howls. This was his looning, — perhaps the wildest sound that is ever heard here, making the woods ring far and wide. I concluded that he laughed in derision of my efforts, confident of his own resources. Though the sky was by this time overcast, the pond was so smooth that I could see where he broke the surface when I did not hear him. His white breast, the stillness of the air, and the smoothness of the water were all against him. At length, having come up fifty rods off, he uttered one of those prolonged howls, as if calling on the god of loons to aid him, and immediately there came a wind from the east and rippled the surface, and filled the whole air with misty rain, and I was impressed as if it were the prayer of the loon answered, and his god was angry with me; and so I left him disappearing far away on the tumultuous surface.

— HENRY DAVID THOREAU, *Walden*

The land retains an identity of its own, still deeper and more subtle than we can know. Our obligation toward it then becomes simple: to approach with an uncalculating mind, with an attitude of regard ... be alert for its openings, for that moment when something sacred reveals itself within the mundane, and you know the land knows you are there.

— BARRY LOPEZ, *Arctic Dreams*

ne moon shows in every pool;
in every pool, the one moon.
— CHINESE PROVERB, 2500 B.C.

ou have noticed that everything an Indian does is in a circle, and that is because the Power of the World always works in circles, and everything tries to be round … The sky is round, and I have heard that the earth is round like a ball, and so are all the stars. The wind, in its greatest power, whirls. Birds make their nests in circles, for theirs is the same religion as ours … Even the seasons form a great circle in their changing, and always come back again to where they were. The life of a man is a circle from childhood to childhood, and so it is in everything where power moves.

— BLACK ELK, OGLALA SIOUX HOLY MAN

The Buddhist scriptures tells us there are eight objections to living in a house: it is a lot of trouble to build; it must be kept in repair; some nobleman might seize it; too many people may want to live in or visit it; it makes the body tender; it provides concealment for committing evil deeds; it causes pride of ownership; and it harbors lice and bugs.

There are ten advantages, on the other hand, in residing under a tree: it can be found with ease; it can be found in any locality; the sight of falling leaves is a reminder of the impermanence of life; a tree arouses no covetous thoughts; it affords no opportunity for evil deeds; it is not received from any person; it is inhabited by good spirits; it needs no fence; it promotes health; it does not involve worldly attachments.

— PUJIMALIYA

nd now, speaking geographically, the end of the Unknown is at hand. This fact in our environment, seemingly as fixed as the wind and the sunset, has at last reached the vanishing point. Is it to be expected that it shall be lost from human experience without something likewise being lost from human character?

I think not. In fact, there is an instinctive human reaction against the loss of fundamental environmental influences, of which history records many examples. The chase, for instance, was a fundamental fact in the life of all nomadic tribes. Again and again, when these tribes conquered and took possession of agricultural regions, where they settled down and became civilized and had no further need of hunting, they nevertheless continued it as a sport, and as such it persists to this day, with ten million devotees in America alone.

It is this same reaction against the loss of adventure into the unknown which causes the hundreds of thousands to sally forth each year upon little expeditions, afoot, by pack train, or by canoe, into the odd bits of wilderness which commerce and "development" have regretfully and temporarily left us here and there. Modest adventurers to be sure, compared with Hanno, or Lewis and Clark. But so is the sportsman, with his setter dog in pursuit of partridges, a modest adventurer compared with his Neolithic ancestor in single combat with the Auroch bull. The point is that along with the necessity for expression of racial instincts there happily goes that capacity for illusion which enables little boys to fish happily in wash-tubs. That capacity is a precious thing, if not overworked.

— ALDO LEOPOLD, *The River of the Mother of God & Other Essays*

All the naturalistic religions are founded
upon the assumption that nature — which
"never did betray the heart that loved her" —
is discoverable and ready to serve as
an infallible guide.

— JOSEPH WOOD KRUTCH

Come on in. The earth, like the sun, like the air, belongs to everyone — and to no one.

— EDWARD ABBEY, *The Journey Home*

*ll birds, even those of the same species, are not alike, and it is the same with animals and with human beings. The reason Wakantanka does not make two birds, or animals, or human beings exactly alike is because each is placed here by Wakantanka to be an independent individuality and to rely upon itself.*

— SHOOTER, TETON SIOUX

A Lakota woman named Elaine Jahner once wrote that what lies at the heart of the religion of hunting peoples is the notion that a spiritual landscape exists within the physical landscape. To put it another way, occasionally one sees something fleeting in the land, a moment when line, color, and movement intensify and something sacred is revealed, leading one to believe that there is another realm of reality corresponding to the physical one but different.

— BARRY LOPEZ, *Arctic Dreams*

 ll things in the world are two. In our minds, we are two — good and evil. With our eyes we see two things — things that are fair and things that are ugly . . . We have the right hand that strikes and makes for evil, and the left hand full of kindness, near the heart. One foot may lead us to an evil way, the other foot may lead us to a good. So are all things two, all two.

— EAGLE CHIEF, PAWNEE

Nature is not benevolent; Nature is just, gives pound for pound, measure for measure, makes no exceptions, never tempers her decrees with mercy, or winks at any infringement of her laws. And in the end is not this best? Could the universe be run as a charity or a benevolent institution, or as a poorhouse of the most approved pattern? Without this merciless justice, this irrefragable law, where should we have brought up long ago? It is a hard gospel; but rocks are hard too, yet they form the foundations of the hills.

— JOHN BURROUGHS, *Time and Change*

Doth not even nature itself teach you.

— *1 Corinthians 11:14*

5

How Much Are the Birds?

nd he cried with a loud voice: Hurt not
the earth, neither the sea, nor the trees.
— *Revelations*

 have been into the lumber-yard, and the carpenter's shop, and the tannery, and the lampblack factory, and the turpentine clearing; but when at length I saw the tops of the pines waving and reflecting the light at a distance high over all the rest of the forest, I realized that the former were not the highest use of the pine. It is not their bones or hide or tallow that I love most. It is the living spirit of the tree, not its spirit of turpentine, with which I sympathize, and which heals my cuts. It is as immortal as I am, and perchance will go to as high a heaven, there to tower above me still.

— HENRY DAVID THOREAU, *The Maine Woods*

The needs of the planet are the needs of the person. And, therefore, the rights of the person are the rights of the planet. If a proper reverence for the sanctity of the Earth and the diversity of its people is the secret of peace and survival, then the adventure of self-discovery stands before us as the most practical of pleasures.

— THEODORE ROSZAK, *Person/Planet*

And God saw everything that he had made, and found it very good. And He said: This is a beautiful world that I have given you. Take good care of it. Do not ruin it.

— FROM A JEWISH PRAYER

Whatever attitude to human existence you fashion for yourself, know that it is valid only if it be the shadow of an attitude to Nature. A human life, so often likened to a spectacle upon a stage, is more justly a ritual. The ancient values of dignity, beauty, and poetry which sustain it are of Nature's inspiration; they are born of the mystery and beauty of the world. Do no dishonour to the earth lest you dishonour the spirit of man. Hold your hands out over the earth as over a flame. To all who loved her, who open to her the doors of their veins, she gives of her strength, sustaining them with her own measureless tremor of dark life. Touch the earth, love the earth, honour the earth, her plains, her valleys, her hills, and her seas; rest your spirit in her solitary places. For the gifts of life are the earth's and they are given to all, and they are the songs of daybreak, Orion and the Bear, and dawn seen over ocean from the beach.

— HENRY BESTON, *The Outermost House*

I do not think that the measure of a civilization is how tall its buildings of concrete are, but rather how well its people have learned to relate to their environment and fellow man.

— SUN BEAR OF THE CHIPPEWA TRIBE

The practice of conservation must spring from a conviction of what is ethically and esthetically right, as well as what is economically expedient. A thing is right only when it tends to preserve the integrity, stability, and beauty of the community, and the community includes the soil, waters, fauna, and flora, as well as people.

It cannot be right, in the ecological sense, for a farmer to drain the last marsh, graze the last woods, or slash the last grove in his community, because in doing so he evicts a fauna, a flora, and a landscape whose membership in the community is older than his own, and is equally entitled to respect.

— ALDO LEOPOLD, *The River of The Mother of God & Other Essays*

One day a child, Honi, saw an old man digging a hole in the earth. Honi asked the man. "Must you do heavy work at your age? Have you no sons to help you?" The man kept digging. "This work I must do myself." Honi asked, "How old are you?" "I am seventy years and seven," answered the man. "And what are you planting?" "I am planting a bread fruit tree," was the answer, "and the fruit of this tree can be made into bread." "And when will your tree bear fruit?" asked Honi. "In seventeen years and seven." "But you surely will not live that long," said Honi. "Yes," said the old man, "I will not live that long, but I must plant this tree. When I came into this world there were trees here for me. It is my duty to make sure that when I leave there will be trees here also."

— OLD JEWISH FOLKTALE

 *he frog does not drink up the pond in which he lives.*

— INDIAN PROVERB

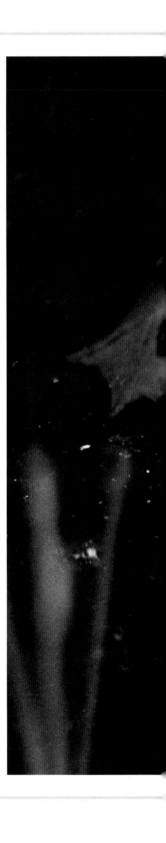

he President in Washington sends word that he wishes to buy our land. But how can you buy or sell the sky? The land? The idea is strange to us. If we do not own the freshness of the air and the sparkle of the water, how can you buy them?

Every part of this earth is sacred to my people. Every shining pine needle, every sandy shore, every mist in the dark woods, every meadow, every humming insect. All are holy in the memory and experience of my people.

We know the sap which courses through the trees as we know the blood that courses through our veins. We are part of the earth and it is part of us. The perfumed flowers are our sisters. The bear, the deer, the great eagle, these are our brothers. The rocky crests, the juices in the meadow, the body heat of the pony, and man, all belong to the same family.

The shining water that moves in the streams and rivers is not just water, but the blood of our ancestors. If we sell you our land, you must remember that it is sacred. Each ghostly reflection in the clear waters of the lakes tells of events and memories in the life of my people. The water's murmur is the voice of my father's father.

The rivers are our brothers. They quench our thirst. They carry our canoes and feed our children. So you must give to the rivers the kindness you would give any brother. If we sell you our land, remember that the air is precious to us, that the air shares its spirit with all the life it supports. The wind that gave our grandfather his first breath also receives his last sigh. The wind also gives our children the spirit of life. So if we sell you our land, you must keep it apart and sacred, as a place where man can go to taste the wind that is sweetened by the meadow flowers.

Will you teach your children what we have taught our children? That the earth is our mother? What befalls the earth befalls all the sons of the earth.

This we know: the earth does not belong to man, man belongs to the earth. All things are connected like the blood that unites us all. Man did not weave the web of life, he is merely a strand in it. Whatever he does to the web, he does to himself.

One thing we know: our god is also your god. The earth is precious to him and to harm the earth is to heap contempt on its creator.

Your destiny is a mystery to us. What will happen when the buffalo are all slaughtered? The wild horses tamed? What will happen when the secret corners of the forest are heavy with the scent of many men and the view of the ripe hills is blotted by talking wires? Where will the thicket be? Gone! Where will the eagle be? Gone! And what is it to say goodbye to the swift pony and the hunt? The end of living and the beginning of survival.

When the last Red Man has vanished with his wilderness and his memory is only the shadow of a cloud moving across the prairie, will these shores and forests still be here?

Will there be any of the spirit of my people left?

We love this earth as a newborn loves its mother's heartbeat. So, if we sell you our land, love it as we have loved it. Care for it as we have cared for it. Hold in your mind the memory of the land as it is when you receive it. Preserve the land for all children and love it, as God loves us all.

As we are part of the land, you too are part of the land. This earth is precious to us. It is also precious to you. One thing we know: there is only one God. No man, be he Red Man or White Man, can be apart. We are brothers after all.

— *The Speech of Chief Seattle*

 country was made to be as we found it. We are the intruders and after we are dead we may have ruined it but it will still be there and we don't know what the next changes are. I suppose they all end up like Mongolia.

— ERNEST HEMINGWAY, *Green Hills of Africa*

Those who would take over the earth
And shape it to their will
Never, I notice, succeed.
The earth is like a vessel so sacred
That at the mere approach of the profane it is marred.
They reach out their fingers and it is gone.

— LAO TZU

In relation to the earth, we have been autistic for centuries. Only now have we begun to listen with some attention and with a willingness to respond to the earth's demands that we cease our industrial assault, that we abandon our inner rage against the conditions of our earthly existence, that we renew our human participation in the grand liturgy of the universe.

— THOMAS BERRY, *The Dream of the Earth*

God was not in the world, then obviously the world was a thing of inferior importance, or of no importance at all. Those who were disposed to exploit it were thus free to do so. And this split in public attitudes was inevitably mirrored in the Lives of individuals: a man could aspire to Heaven with his mind and his heart while destroying the earth, and his fellow men, with his hands ... This contempt for the world or the hatred of it ... has reached a terrifying climax in our own time. The rift between body and soul, the Creator and the Creation, has admitted the entrance into the world of machinery of the world's doom.

— WENDELL BERRY, *A Secular Pilgrimage*

y plucking her petals, you do not gather the beauty of the flower.

—RABINDRANATH TAGORE

USED TROUT STREAM FOR SALE.
MUST BE SEEN TO BE APPRECIATED.

I went inside and looked at some ship's lanterns that were for sale next to the door. Then a salesman came up to me and said in a pleasant voice, "Can I help you?"

"Yes," I said. "I'm curious about the trout stream you have for sale. Can you tell me something about it? How are you selling it?"

"We're selling it by the foot length. You can buy as little as you want or you can buy all we've got left. A man came in here this morning and bought 563 feet. He's going to give it to his niece for a birthday present," the salesman said.

"We're selling the waterfalls separately of course, and the trees and birds, flowers, grass and ferns we're also selling extra. The insects we're giving away free with a minimum purchase of ten feet of stream."

"How much are you selling the stream for?" I asked.

"Six dollars and fifty-cents a foot," he said. "That's for the first hundred feet. After that it's five dollars a foot."

"How much are the birds?" I asked.

"Thirty-five cents apiece," he said. "But of course they're used. We can't guarantee anything."

"How wide is the stream?" I asked. "You said you were selling it by the length, didn't you?"

"Yes," he said. "We're selling it by the length. Its width runs between five and eleven feet. You don't have to pay anything extra for width. It's not a big stream, but it's very pleasant."

"What kinds of animals do you have?" I asked.

"We only have three deer left," he said.

"Oh ... What about flowers ?"

"By the dozen," he said.

"Is the stream clear?" I asked.

"Sir," the salesman said. "I wouldn't want you to think that we would ever sell a murky trout stream here. We always make sure they're running crystal clear before we even think about moving them."

"Where did the stream come from?" I asked.

"Colorado," he said. "We moved it with loving care. We've never damaged a trout stream yet. We treat them all as if they were china."

"You're probably asked this all the time, but how's fishing in the stream?" I asked.

"Very good," he said. "Mostly German browns, but there are a few rainbows."

"What do the trout cost?" I asked.

"They come with the stream," he said. "Of course it's all luck. You never know how many you're going to get or how big they are. But the fishing's very good, you might say it's excellent. Both bait and dry fly," he said smiling.

"Where's the stream at?" I asked. "I'd like to take a look at it."

"It's around in back," he said. "You go straight through that door and then turn right until you're outside. It's stacked in lengths. You can't miss it. The waterfalls are upstairs in the used plumbing department."

"What about the animals?"

"Well, what's left of the animals are straight back from the stream. You'll see a bunch of our trucks parked on a road by the railroad tracks. Turn right on the road and follow it down past the piles of lumber. The animal shed's right at the end of the lot."

"Thanks," I said. "I think I'll look at the waterfalls first. You don't have to come with me. Just tell me how to get there and I'll find my own way."

"All right," he said. "Go up those stairs. You'll see a bunch of doors and windows, turn left and you'll find the used plumbing department. Here's my card if you need any help."

"Okay," I said. "You've been a great help already. Thanks a lot. I'll take a look around."

"Good luck," he said.

I went upstairs and there were thousands of doors there. I'd never seen so many doors before in my life. You could have built an entire city out of those doors. Doorstown. And there were enough windows up there to build a little suburb entirely out of windows. Windowville.

I turned left and went back and saw the faint glow of pearl colored light. The light got stronger and stronger as I went farther back, and then I was in the used plumbing department, surrounded by hundreds of toilets.

The toilets were stacked on shelves. They were stacked five toilets high. There was a skylight above the toilets that made them glow like the Great Taboo Pearl of the South Sea movies.

Stacked over against the wall were the waterfalls. There were about a dozen of them, ranging from a drop of a few feet to a drop of ten or fifteen feet.

There was one waterfall that was over sixty feet long. There were tags on the pieces of the big falls describing the correct order for putting the falls back together again.

The waterfalls all had price tags on them. They were more expensive than the stream. The waterfalls were selling for $19.00 a foot.

I went into another room where there were piles of sweet smelling lumber, glowing a soft yellow from a different color skylight above the lumber. In the shadows at the edge of the room under the sloping roof of the building were many sinks and urinals covered with dust, and there was also another waterfall about seventeen feet long, lying there in two lengths and already beginning to gather dust.

I had seen all I wanted of the waterfalls, and now I was very curious about the trout stream, so I followed the salesman's directions and ended up outside the building.

O I had never in my life seen anything like that trout stream. It was stacked in piles of various lengths: ten, fifteen, twenty feet, etc. There was one pile of hundred-foot lengths. There was also a box of scraps. The scraps were in odd sizes ranging from six inches to a couple of feet.

There was a loudspeaker on the side of the building and soft music was coming out.

It was a cloudy day and seagulls were circling high overhead.

Behind the stream were big bundles of trees and bushes. They were covered with sheets of patched canvas. You could see the tops and roots sticking out the ends of the bundles.

I went up close and looked at the lengths of stream. I could see some trout in them. I saw one good fish. I saw some crawdads crawling around the rocks at the bottom.

It looked like a fine stream. I put my hand in the water. It was cold and felt good.

I decided to go around to the side and look at the animals. I saw where the trucks were parked beside the railroad tracks. I followed the road down past the piles of lumber, back to the shed where the animals were.

The salesman had been right. They were practically out of animals. About the only thing they had left in any abundance were mice. There were hundreds of mice.

Beside the shed was a huge wire birdcage, maybe fifty feet high, filled with many kinds of birds. The top of the cage had a piece of canvas over it, so the birds wouldn't get wet when it rained. There were woodpeckers and wild canaries and sparrows.

On my way back to where the trout stream was piled, I found the insects. They were inside a prefabricated steel building that was selling for eighty-cents a square foot. There was a sign over the door. It said INSECTS.

— RICHARD BRAUTIGAN, *The Cleveland Wrecking Yard*

It is a soul-shattering silence. You hold your breath and hear absolutely nothing. No rustling of leaves in the wind, no rumbling of distant traffic, no chatter of birds or insects or children. You are alone with God in that silence. There in the white flat silence I began for the first time to feel a slight sense of shame for what we were proposing to do. Did we really intend to invade this silence with our trucks and bulldozers and after a few years leave it a radioactive junkyard?

— FREEMAN DYSON, *Disturbing the Universe*

ut even as we glance over the grimy world before us, the sun shines radiantly over the earth, the aspen leaves shimmer in the evening breeze, the coo of the mourning dove and the swelling chorus of the insects fill the land, while down in the hollows the mist deepens the fragrance of the honeysuckle.

— THOMAS BERRY, *The Dream of the Earth*

6

A Child of the Universe

You are a child of the universe, no less than the trees & the stars; you have a right to be here. And whether or not it is clear to you, no doubt the universe is unfolding as it should.

— *Desiderata*

o everything there is a season, and a time to every purpose under the heaven.

— *Ecclesiastes*

I am going to venture that the man who sat on the ground in his tipi meditating on life and its meaning, accepting the kinship of all creatures, and acknowledging unity with the universe of things was infusing into his being the true essence of civilization.

— LUTHER STANDING BEAR, OGLALA SIOUX CHIEF

Standing there alone, I felt alive, more aware and receptive than ever before. A shout or a movement would have destroyed the spell. This was a time for silence, for being in pace with ancient rhythms and timelessness, the breathing of the lake, the slow growth of living things. Here the cosmos could be felt and the true meaning of attunement.

— SIGURD F. OLSON, *The Singing Wilderness*

This afternoon, I have found quiet hours alone picking tomatoes. As my fingers find ripe tomatoes, red and firm, through the labyrinth of leaves, I am absorbed into the present. My garden asks nothing more of me than I am able to give. I pull tomatoes, gently placing them in the copper colander. Pulling tomatoes. Pulling tomatoes. Some come easily.

— TERRY TEMPEST WILLIAMS, *Refuge*

The mountains, I become part of it . . .
The herbs, the fir tree, I become part of it.
The morning mists, the clouds, the gathering waters,
I become part of it.
The wilderness, the dew drops, the pollen . . .
I become part of it.

— NAVAJO CHANT

e all travel the milky way together, trees and men; but it never occurred to me until this storm-day, while swinging in the wind, that trees are travelers, in the ordinary sense. They make many journeys, not extensive ones, it is true; but our own little journeys, away and back again, are only little more than tree-wavings — many of them not so much.

When the storm began to abate, I dismounted and sauntered down through the calming woods. The storm-tones died away, and, turning toward the east, I beheld the countless hosts of the forests hushed and tranquil, towering above one another on the slopes of the hills like a devout audience. The setting sun filled them with amber light, and seemed to say, while they listened, "My peace I give unto you."

As I gazed upon the impressive scene, all the so-called ruin of the storm was forgotten, and never before did these noble woods appear so fresh, so joyous, so immortal.

— JOHN MUIR,
The Mountains of California

Be like a tree in pursuit of your cause.
Stand firm, grip hard, thrust upward, bend to
the winds of heaven, and learn tranquility.

— DEDICATION TO RICHARD ST. BARBE BAKER, FATHER OF THE TREES

know the solitude my mother speaks of. It is what sustains me and protects me from my mind. It renders me fully present. I am desert. I am mountains. I am Great Salt Lake. There are other languages being spoken by wind, water, and wings. There are other lives to consider: avocets, stilts, and stones. Peace is the perspective found in patterns. When I see ring-billed gulls picking on the flesh of decaying carp, I am less afraid of death. We are no more and no less than the life that surrounds us. My fears surface in my isolation. My serenity surfaces in my solitude.

— TERRY TEMPEST WILLIAMS, *Refuge*

he knowledge that my individual life is but a span, a breath; that in a little while I too must wither and mingle like one of those fallen leaves with the mould, does not grieve me. I know it and yet disbelieve it; for am I not here alive, where men have inhabited for thousands of years, feeling what I now feel — their oneness with everlasting nature and the undying human family?

— W. H. HUDSON, *Afoot in England*

To speak truly, few adult persons can see nature ... The lover of nature is he whose inward and outward senses are truly adjusted to each other; who has retained the spirit of infancy even into the era of manhood ... In the woods ... a man casts off his years as the snake his slough, and at what period soever of life is always a child. In the woods is perpetual youth. Within these plantations of God, a decorum and a sanctity reign, a perennial festival is dressed, and the guest sees not how he should tire of them in a thousand years. In the woods we return to reason and faith. There I feel that nothing can befall me in life, — no disgrace, no calamity (leaving me my eyes), which nature cannot repair. Standing on the bare ground ... the currents of the Universal Being circulate through me; I am part or parcel of God.

— RALPH WALDO EMERSON, "NATURE"

The Lord is my shepherd; I shall not want.
He maketh me to lie down in green pastures:
he leadeth me beside the still waters.

— *Psalm 23*

 virtuous man when alone loves the quiet of the mountains.
A wise man in nature enjoys the purity of water.
One must not be suspicious of the fool who takes pleasure in mountains and streams.
But rather measure how well he sharpens his spirit by them.

— MURO MUSEK, 14TH CENTURY ZEN MASTER

We are nearer heaven when we listen to the birds than when we quarrel with our fellow men. I am sure that none can enter into the spirit of Christ, His evangel, save those who willingly follow His invitation when He says, "Come ye yourselves apart into this lonely place, and rest a while." For since His blessed kingdom was first established in the green fields, by the lakeside, with humble fishermen for its subjects, the easiest way into it hath ever been through the wicket-gate of a lowly and grateful fellowship with nature. He that feels not the beauty and blessedness and peace of the woods and meadows that God hath bedecked with flowers for him even while he is yet a sinner, how shall he learn to enjoy the unfading bloom of the celestial country if he ever becomes a saint?

— HENRY VAN DYKE, *The Gentle Life*

hen a spider makes a beautiful web, the beauty comes out of the spider's nature. It's instinctive beauty. How much of the beauty of our own lives is about the beauty of being alive? How much of it is conscious and intentional? That is a big question.

— JOSEPH CAMPBELL, *The Power of Myth*

noiseless patient spider,
I mark'd where on a little promontory it stood isolated
Mark'd how to explore the vacant vast surrounding,
It launch'd forth filament, filament, filament, out of itself,
Ever unreeling them, ever tirelessly speeding them.

And you O my soul where you stand,
Surrounded, detached, in measureless oceans of space,
Ceaselessly musing, venturing, throwing, seeking the spheres to connect them,
Till the bridge you will need be form'd, till the ductile anchor hold,
Till the gossamer thread you fling catch somewhere, O my soul.

— WALT WHITMAN

If the heart were right, then every creature would be a mirror of life and a book of holy
doctrine. There is no creature so small and abject but it reflects the goodness of God.

— THOMAS A. KEMPIS

At last I am beginning to believe I am part of all this life and to know how I evolved from
the primal dust to a creature capable of seeing beauty. This is compensation enough. No
one can ever take this dream away; it will be with me until the day I have seen my last
sunset, and listened for a final time to the wind whispering through the pines.

— SIGURD F. OLSON, *Reflections From the North Country*

*Hidden Life, vibrant in every atom,*
O Hidden Light, shining in every creature,
O Hidden Love, embracing all in Oneness,
May each who feels himself as one with Thee
Know he is therefore one with every other.

— ANNIE BESANT

We are here to witness the creation and to abet it. We are here to notice each thing so each thing gets noticed. Together we notice not only each mountain shadow and each stone on the beach but, especially, we notice the beautiful faces and complex natures of each other. We are here to bring to consciousness the beauty and power that are around us and to praise the people who are here with us. We witness our generation and our times. We watch the weather. Otherwise, creation would be playing to an empty house.

— ANNIE DILLARD, *The Meaning of Life*

Who shall describe the inexpressible tenderness and immortal life of the grim forest, where Nature, though it be mid-winter, is ever in her spring, where the moss-grown and decaying trees are not old, but seem to enjoy a perpetual youth; and blissful, innocent Nature, like a serene infant, is too happy to make a noise, except by a few tinkling, lisping birds and trickling rills?

What a place to live, what a place to die and be buried in! There certainly men would live forever, and laugh at death and the grave. There they could have no such thoughts as are associated with the village graveyard, — that make a grave out of one of those moist evergreen hummocks !

— HENRY DAVID THOREAU, *The Maine Woods*

The longer I live the more my mind dwells upon the beauty and the wonder of the world ... I have loved the feel of the grass under my feet, and the sound of the running streams by my side. The hum of the wind in the treetops has always been good music to me, and the face of the fields has often comforted me more than the faces of men. I am in love with this world.

— JOHN BURROUGHS,
The Summit of the Years

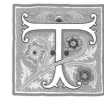

This stream floweth wimping and laughing down to the great sea which it knoweth not; yet it doth not fret because the future is hidden; and doubtless it were wise in us to accept the mysteries of life as cheerfully and go forward with a merry heart, considering that we know enough to make us happy and keep us honest for day. A man should be well content if he can see so far ahead of him as the next bend in the stream. What lies beyond, let him trust in the hand of God.

— HENRY VAN DYKE,
The Ruling Passion

 hen the sun rises, I go to work. When the sun goes down, I take my rest, I dig the well from which I drink, I farm the soil which yields my food, I share creation, Kings can do no more.

— ANCIENT CHINESE PROVERB, 2500 B.C.

 nd this, our life, exempt from public haunt, finds tongues in trees, books in the running brooks, sermons in stones, and good in everything.

— WILLIAM SHAKESPEARE

I think I could turn and live with animals, they are so placid and self-contain'd,
I stand and look at them long and long.
They do not sweat and whine about their condition,
They do not alike awake in the dark and weep for their sins,
They do not make me sick discussing their duty to God,
Not one is dissatisfied, not one is demented with the mania of owning things,
Not one kneels to another, nor to his kind that lived thousands of years ago,
Not one is respectable or unhappy over the whole earth.
So they show their relations to me and I accept them,
They bring me tokens of myself, they evince them plainly in their possession.
I wonder where they get those tokens,
Did I pass that way huge times ago and negligently drop them?

— WALT WHITMAN

The outer world, from which we cower into our houses, seemed
after all a gentle habitable place; and night after night a man's
bed, it seemed, was laid and waiting for him in the fields, where
God keeps an open house.

— ROBERT LOUIS STEVENSON, *Travels with a Donkey*

he burdened earth is sprinkled by the rain,
The winds blow cool, the lightnings roam on high.
Eased and allayed th'obsessions of the mind,
And in my heart the spirit's mastery.
— *Theragatha, Psalm 50, Pali Canon, Buddhist Spirituality*

Mounting toward the upland again, I pause reverently, as the hush and stillness of twilight come upon the woods. It is the sweetest, ripest hour of the day. And as the hermit's evening hymn goes up from the deep solitude below me, I experience that serene exaltation of sentiment of which music, literature, and religion are but the faint types and symbols.
— JOHN BURROUGHS, *Wake Robin*

Great Spirit, Great Spirit, my Grandfather, all over the earth the faces of living things are alike ... Look upon these faces of children without number and with children in their arms, that they may face the winds and walk the good rood to the day of quiet.

— BLACK ELK, OGLALA SIOUX HOLY MAN

It is the bounty of nature that we live, but of philosophy, that we live well, which is, in truth, a greater benefit than life itself.

— SENECA

Last year in a lovely temple in Hirosawa
This year among the rocks of Nikko
All's the same to me;
Clapping hands, the peaks roar at the blue.

— SATORI POEM BY HAKUGAI, 13TH CENTURY

*evertheless the flowers*
fall with our attachment
And the weeds spring up
with our aversion.

— DOGEN

It is amazing that no one ever questions the truth of the story of a lost Paradise. How beautiful, after all, was the Garden of Eden, and how ugly, after all, is the present physical universe? Have flowers ceased to bloom since Eve and Adam sinned? Has God cursed the apple tree and forbidden it to bear fruit because one man sinned, or has He decided that its blossoms should be made of duller or paler colors? Have orioles and nightingales and skylarks ceased to sing? Is there no snow upon the mountain tops and are there no reflections in the lakes? Are there no rosy sunsets today and no rainbows and no haze nestling over villages, and are there no falling cataracts and gurgling streams and shady trees? Who therefore invented the myth that the "Paradise" was "lost" and that today we are living in an ugly universe? We are indeed ungrateful spoiled children of God.

— LIN YUTANG,
The Importance of Living

f this little world tonight
Suddenly should fall through space
In a hissing, headlong flight,
Shrivelling from off its face,
As it falls into the sun,
In an instant every trace
Of the little crawling things —
Ants, philosophers, and lice,
Cattle, cockroaches and kings,
Beggars, millionaires and mice,
Men and maggots — all as one
As it falls into the sun —
Who can say but at the same
Instant from some planet far
A child may watch us and exclaim:
"See the pretty shooting star!"

— HERFORD

SOURCE NOTES AND COPYRIGHT NOTICES